Hugo Sánchez

To the Top!

2010 Awarded the Golden Foot.

2006 Hired as the coach for the Mexican national team.

2000 Begins coaching, starting with the Pumas.

1997 Retires as a player.

1994 Plays in his last World Cup.

1992 Begins playing for Club América.

1990 Awarded the Golden Boot for making the most goals of any player in Europe.

1989 Wins King's Cup with Real Madrid.

1986 Mexico hosts World Cup and wins sixth place.

1985 Signs with Real Madrid; wins UEFA Cup; wins first Pichichi trophy.

1981 Begins playing for Atlético Madrid.

1978 Plays in first World Cup.

1976 Plays in the Olympics; begins playing for the Pumas.

1975 Wins the World Youth Cup with the national Mexican youth team.

1958 On July 11, Hugo Sánchez is born in Mexico City.

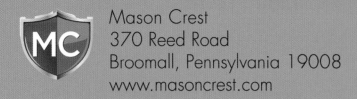

Mason Crest
370 Reed Road
Broomall, Pennsylvania 19008
www.masoncrest.com

Printed and bound in the United States of America.

First printing
9 8 7 6 5 4 3 2 1

Series ISBN: 978-1-4222-2647-6
ISBN: 978-1-4222-2668-1
ebook ISBN: 978-1-4222-9209-9

Library of Congress Cataloging-in-Publication Data

Martínez Alaníz, Eduardo.
  Hugo Sánchez / by Eduardo Martínez Alaníz.
     p. cm.
  ISBN 978-1-4222-2668-1 (hardback) – ISBN 978-1-4222-2647-6 (series hardback) – ISBN 978-1-4222-9209-9 (ebook)
  1. Sánchez, Hugo, 1958–Juvenile literature. 2. Soccer players–Mexico–Biography–Juvenile literature. I. Title.
  GV942.7.S24M37 2013
  796.334092–dc23
  [B]
                                        2012030252

ABOUT THE AUTHOR:
EDUARDO MARTÍNEZ ALANÍZ was born in Buenos Aires, Argentina. He currently lives in Birmingham, Alabama where he broadcasts for different radio stations in the southeastern United States. He's also written sports columns for several local magazines and covered sports events for GSM Communications and Atlanta's sports newspaper *Contra Ataque* in Georgia, United States.

PICTURE CREDITS:
EFE Photos: 1, 4, 6, 8, 10, 11, 12, 13, 14, 15, 16, 18, 20, 22, 23, 24, 26, 27, 28

SUPERSTARS OF SOCCER

Hugo Sánchez

CONTENTS

CHAPTER 1

A Golden Child

Mexico has turned out a lot of soccer stars over the years. Hugo Sánchez is one of the most famous. He is known as the "Golden Child," among other things. Not only does he play great soccer in Mexico, he also played on one of the best teams in the world—Spain's Real Madrid. Both in Mexico and around the world, Sánchez draws the attention of fans everywhere.

HUGO'S DRIVE

Hugo Sánchez was born in Mexico City on July 11, 1958. His father was also a **PROFESSIONAL** soccer player. Since his father loved the sport so much, it's not a surprise that Hugo started playing when he was very young.

Sánchez's first soccer school was on the streets and fields of his neighborhood. He and the other local kids played all the time. Sánchez became a better player by playing with kids who were three or four years older.

Even at the age of eleven, Hugo was already a great player. People started to notice his skills. Some predicted he would be a pro, just like his father.

Hugo almost didn't become a soccer player, though. First, he went to school to become a dentist. But while there, he still played soccer. In the end, Hugo chose a career in soccer over cleaning teeth.

It wasn't long before Hugo was making big news. In 1975, he played for the national Mexican youth team. Sánchez and his team won the World Youth Cup that year. He played so well during the Cup that he earned the nickname Golden Child. People thought he was the best player on the team. He also won the Pan-American Championship that same year.

Sánchez's goal was to get on the adult national team. He wanted to make it to the Olympic Games. He trained and studied for three years. He got up at

Sánchez does his trademark backflip after making a goal.

six in the morning to practice, and studied until ten at night. He was driven to reach his goal!

All that hard work paid off. While he was still just a teenager, Sánchez was picked to be part of the Mexican national team. He played in the Olympic Games in Montreal in 1976. He also won the Confederation of North, Central American, and Caribbean Football Associations (CONCACAF) tournament.

In all, Hugo played eighty international matches by the time he was eighteen. He played well in those matches, too. Sánchez scored sixty goals in that time. He was ready for the next step.

QUITE A PLAYER

Hugo Sánchez is a great player for two reasons. First, he scores a lot. Second, he's always in great shape. He brought both of those things to his first adult team.

When he was eighteen years old, Sánchez started playing for a team called the Pumas. The Pumas are from the national university in Mexico. Sánchez joined the team because he was at university to become a dentist.

The Pumas weren't very good before Sánchez joined the team. They hadn't won many **CHAMPIONSHIPS** or trophies. That would all change with their new player.

Right away, Sánchez made a difference. During his first season, the Pumas won their first Mexican League Championship.

Sánchez didn't only play soccer in Mexico. He wanted to play as much as he could. During the **OFF-SEASON** in Mexico, he played with the San Diego Sockers in the United States.

Back in Mexico for the 1978–1979 season, Sánchez stood out as a star on the Pumas. He was one of the highest scorers in the Mexican league. He had twenty-six goals. He started earning his nickname "Hugol," or "Hu-goal," in Spanish.

With Sánchez in the lead, the Pumas played with all their strength. They were CONCACAF champions. They also won the International Cup in 1981.

In his six seasons with the Pumas, Sánchez scored ninety-nine goals. At the same time, Mexican fans grew to know and love the young star. They started to expect that he would score at just about every game. And most of the time, he didn't let the fans down.

It Runs in the Family

The Sánchez family is very athletic. Hugo's father was a professional soccer player in Mexico and Spain. His sister is also an athlete. In fact, she competed in the same Olympic Games that Hugo first played in. His sister, Herlinda, is a gymnast. She taught him how to somersault. Whenever Sánchez made a great goal, he would pull out the trick that Herlinda taught him. Fans got to know Sánchez for his trademark somersault on the field.

Fans got to know the face of Hugo Sánchez during his star years in Mexico and Spain.

CHAPTER 2

Pentapichichi

Hugo Sánchez's skills were getting a lot of attention from people in Mexico. His fame was also spreading around the world.

Soccer experts in Europe started looking at Sánchez. Some offered him contracts. Sánchez ended up with the Atlético from Madrid. His first season started in 1981. Sánchez knew he had a lot to live up to. Could he do it?

BECOMING A STAR

A lot of people didn't have faith in the young Mexican player. They were used to big stars that could score a lot. At first, Sánchez didn't do so well. He had some ups and downs, but didn't play as well as he knew he could.

Finally, a few years in, Sánchez found his stride. During the 1984–85 season, he started playing like he knew he could. He and the Atlético were second place in the Spanish league. Then they won the King's Cup, the Spanish championship game.

Sánchez also won his first Pichichi trophy. The award is given to the highest-scoring player in the league. Sánchez had scored nineteen goals during one season. No one else beat him.

The Pichichi trophy was the first of several. During his career, he ended up winning five of them. That's why he's called "Pentapichichi" ("penta" means five).

Sánchez played with the Atlético for a few years. Then he moved on to his next team. For a brief time, he returned to Mexico to play for the Pumas again. After that, Sánchez moved to one of the best teams in the world—Real Madrid in Spain. Playing for the Spanish team was a dream come true.

With Real Madrid, Sánchez had the best years in his career. During his very first season with the team, he won the championship in the Spanish league. He was also the highest scorer again, and won another Pichichi trophy. Sánchez was at the height of his soccer career.

The list kept going and the awards kept coming. Real Madrid and Sánchez won the Union of European Football Associations (UEFA) Cup in 1985. The

team also won the King's Cup in 1989 and the Super Cup in 1991.

Real Madrid was almost unstoppable. Sánchez was one of the team's top **FORWARDS.** He played with other big stars. A group of players called "La Quinta del Buitre" ("The Vultures") were part of Real Madrid with Sánchez. The Vultures were five Spanish soccer stars that helped the team win again and again.

Sánchez himself did great things while playing for Real Madrid. He scored thirty-four goals in the 1987 season alone. In 1988, he made twenty-nine. In 1990, he scored an amazing thirty-eight, tying the record.

In 1990, Sánchez won the Golden Boot. The Boot is given to the player who has scored the most goals in all of Europe! In 2010, Cristiano Ronaldo was the first player to break Sánchez's record of thirty-eight goals. Right before Ronaldo broke the record, Sánchez said, "I'll celebrate…records were made to be beat."

In all, Sánchez played for seven seasons with Real Madrid. He played in 240 league matches. In all those games, he scored 164 goals and won four more Pichichis.

Sánchez earned some attention with the Pumas.

While Sánchez was playing for Spanish teams, he continued to play on the Mexican national team—the Tri.

The Mexican League

Mexican professional soccer has been around since 1943. It started with ten clubs, and has grown since then. Mexican soccer is split into divisions. The First Division is made up of the top teams and players. Each year, there are two championships, the Apertura (Opening) in the winter, and the Clausura (Closing) in the summer.

After the end of each season, the worst team from the First Division is moved down to the Second. The best team in the Second Division is also moved up to the First Division. Moving teams to different divisions keeps the competition between teams interesting.

Sánchez holds one of the many cups he's earned with his teams over the years.

The Golden Child makes an amazing kick.

WHAT IS THE SUPER CUP?

The Super Cup is a championship game in Europe. Every year, it is played by the champion of the UEFA Europa League and the champion of the UEFA Champions League. They are the two top leagues in Europe. The Cup is only one game long, and determines the best team in Europe for that year. Sánchez's team Real Madrid most recently played the Super Cup in 2011, but the team lost to Barcelona.

AFTER THE REAL

Up until 1990, Sánchez had been in the best shape he could be. He hadn't had to sit out much, and he hadn't been hurt while playing. Then, during the 1990–91 season, **INJURIES** put him on the bench. Sánchez couldn't play for almost a year.

Even after Sánchez came back to soccer, things were rough. He got in trouble with Real Madrid, and the team punished him. It was clear that Sánchez and Real Madrid weren't getting along anymore.

Real Madrid poses after their UEFA Cup victory.

Sánchez decided to leave the team. He definitely wasn't ready to retire, though. After leaving Real Madrid, he traveled around from team to team, trying to find a good fit. First, he played for Club América in Mexico. He even won the CONCACAF Champions Cup with the team.

Sánchez's real goal was to play in Europe again. After América, he played for the Rayo Vallecano. That made him one of the few non-Spanish athletes to play for three Spanish clubs. All three teams play in the Spanish capital of Madrid.

Sánchez played twenty-nine games for his new Spanish team. He played very well and scored sixteen goals during that time. When the star of the team, Perez Michu, was compared to Sánchez, he said, "[That's a] huge compliment. You are naming a major soccer player, and it is an honor to be among them."

Sánchez didn't stay with one team long, though. He played for Atlante in Mexico for a little while. Then he played for an Austrian team called FC Keli Linz. The team played in the second division. Sánchez ended up winning the championship with FC Keli Linz. He also helped the team move up a division.

Next, Sánchez played for FC Dallas in the United States. The Mexican soccer superstar didn't stay with Dallas for very long, though. At the end of a year, he had played for four teams in four different countries!

Sánchez may have goofed off on the field from time to time, but he knew when he had to focus.

Hugo Sánchez is no stranger to awards.

CHAPTER 3

Hugo and the Tri

While Hugo Sánchez has spent a lot of time playing for other countries, he still played for Mexico, too. Sánchez was a part of the Mexican national team for many years. Though he's been all over the world, Mexico is still Sánchez's home.

The Mexican national team is known as the "Tri." The nickname refers to the three colors on the team's uniform. Sánchez and many other great players have worn the team's red, white, and green uniforms over the years.

WORLD CUPS

Sánchez first wore the Mexican uniform in 1975. He played in the World Youth Cup. In the end, his team won. Teams from countries all over the world played in the World Youth Cup. Sánchez had gotten his first taste of playing soccer at an international level.

Sánchez stayed on the team over the next few years. In 1977, he played in **QUALIFYING** World Cup games. He scored his first goal just thirty-three seconds into his first game with the team. Sánchez helped his team win five matches in the **TOURNAMENT.** The Mexican national team was headed to the 1978 World Cup.

Sánchez did so well, that he earned himself a place as a starter on Mexico's national team. The average age of the team was just twenty-two. It was the youngest Mexican team to ever play in the World Cup.

The team didn't do as well as fans had hoped, though. Some thought the team was too young. Mexico ended up leaving the World Cup early.

In 1986, Mexico made it to the World Cup again. This time, the huge event was hosted by Mexico. The national team had a spot in the Cup, but the team wanted to make sure they did well. The Tri wanted to prove to the world that they were a good team.

Mexico did very well in the 1986 World Cup. They beat Belgium 2–1. Then they tied with Paraguay 1–1. The team also beat Iraq 1–0, although Sánchez didn't play in that game.

Eventually, Sánchez would coach the national team that he once played for.

In the pre-quarterfinals, Mexico again came out on top, beating Bulgaria. Finally, they lost to Germany, which was a very strong team. Mexico ended up in sixth place, which was the best the country had ever finished in the World Cup.

In 1994, Sánchez played in his last World Cup. The Cup was held in the United States. Sánchez knew it would be his last World Cup because he was thirty-three. He would be too old for the next one.

Mexico had a shaky start in the tournament. But the team ended up making it past the first round. Sánchez didn't get to play in the pre-quarterfinals against Bulgaria. Mexico lost the match.

The 1994 World Cup was the last that Sánchez played with the Tri.

THE AMERICA CUP

The America Cup is a championship in South America. A few teams from other parts of the world are invited each year to play with the South American teams. In 1993, Mexico was invited to play in the Cup for the first time.

Mexico lost its first game. In the team's second game, the Tri tied Argentina. Sánchez earned an assist in that game.

Soon, Mexico made it to the finals by winning against Ecuador. Ecuador hadn't lost a single game in the tournament until losing to Mexico. Sánchez scored one of the two Mexican goals against Ecuador.

Mexico faced Argentina in the finals. Mexico lost the game, but the Tri had done very well in its first America Cup.

Some fans thought that Sánchez should have done more to make the Tri a great team. He was so good on his other teams. Many fans thought Sánchez was one of the best players ever. Why hadn't Mexico won a World Cup? Why hadn't the team won more championships? No one player can win a World Cup, of course. Sánchez was just one person. A team must work together to become great.

Sánchez didn't win the World Cup with the Mexican national team, but he still did a lot of good for the team. He played in fifty-eight official matches, and scored twenty-nine goals.

In 1997, Sánchez played his last official game. In his final game, he simply touched the ball and walked off the field. His time as a player was over. Fans everywhere were sad to see him go, but they hadn't seen the last of the Golden Child.

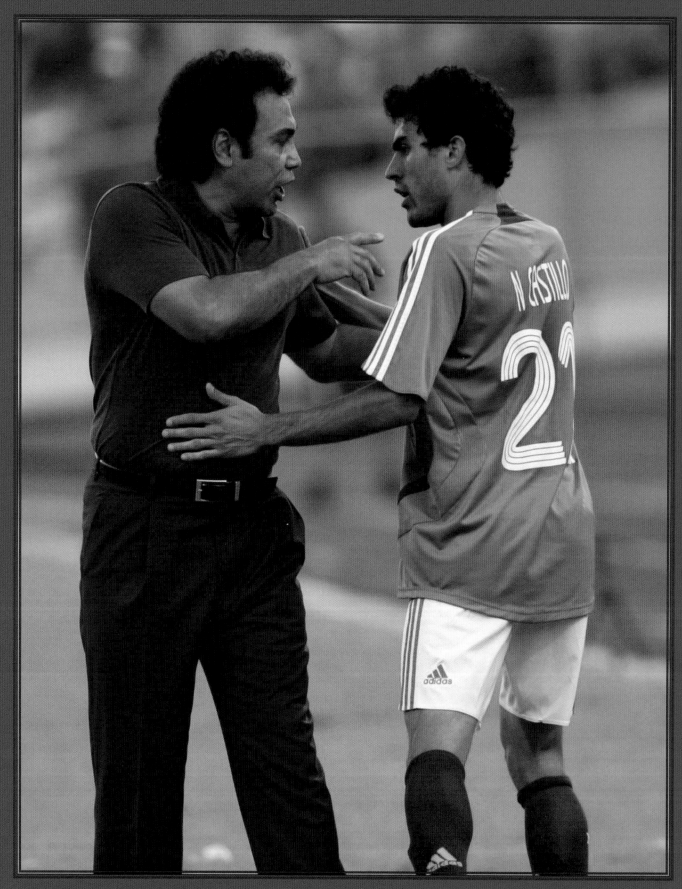

Sánchez gives a player advice as coach.

CHAPTER 4

From Player to Coach

Not every big player becomes a great coach. There's a big difference between playing well and coaching well. You have to know how to talk to players, plan, and think on your feet. Hugo Sánchez does.

After finishing his time as a player, Hugo Sánchez made the move from star to coach. Although he hasn't always been the best coach, he has poured his love of the game into his new position.

HELLO AND GOODBYE TO THE PUMAS

Sánchez couldn't stay away from soccer forever. After he stopped playing, he decided to try his hand at coaching. Sánchez started coaching the same team he started his soccer career with. In 2000, he began coaching the Pumas in Mexico. Sánchez took the team to the 2000 Summer Tournament. The team made it to the **PLAYOFFS.**

Sánchez didn't get along with the president of the club. The soccer star left coaching the Pumas for a while. He wanted to wait until the president moved on. In 2001, the club's president left the team, so Sánchez came back to coach the Pumas.

With Sánchez coaching, the Pumas did very well. In 2004, the team won both tournaments for the year, the Opening and the Closing.

Although the team had a lot of stars, Sánchez's coaching was a big part of the team. He drove the players to do their best. The team ended up winning two championships!

Unfortunately, things weren't so great the next year. The Pumas didn't play well in 2005 and ended up last in the league. After the bad season, Sánchez decided to leave the team.

Sánchez wasn't ready to give up coaching, though. He told fans that he was still learning about soccer and about himself. He said that he was still getting better as a coach.

A DREAM COME TRUE

Sánchez was ready for the next challenge. In 2006, he was hired as the

coach for the Mexican national team, which was a big honor and a big responsibility.

Sánchez was going to make a lot of money coaching the Tri. His pay was over $1 million! Sánchez would have to work hard for that money, though. His job was to help the team win big. As coach, he would have to take the Tri to the semifinals in the America Cup. He'd also have to take the team to the Olympics and win a medal.

Sánchez coached his first game with the Tri in February 2007. Sadly, the team lost the game.

Right away, fans started to worry about Sánchez's coaching. To prove them wrong, Sánchez worked hard to win the next few games. But even that didn't make people stop talking. Many fans didn't like how he was coaching.

Even with all the worry from fans, the national team made it to the

Sánchez didn't always get his team to win big, but he tried hard.

Sánchez now had to lead the Mexican team he had played on for so many years.

America Cup in 2007. First, Mexico defeated Brazil 2–0. In the next game, the Tri beat Ecuador. Next, Mexico won against Paraguay, 6–0. The team finally lost a game to Argentina. That meant the team had to play Uruguay for third place in the Cup. The Tri easily defeated Uruguay 3–1.

The America Cup was a shining moment for Sánchez and the team. They had done well, and Sánchez had led his team to a win!

Next, Sánchez would have to take his team to the Olympics. Sadly for Sánchez, Mexico didn't do as well as the team needed to. Everyone thought that the Tri would at least qualify for the Olympics. Instead, the team lost in the Pre-Olympic trials in the United States. Fans were unhappy. Sánchez was fired before the Olympics even started.

But his poor job as a coach didn't get in the way of fans remembering Sánchez as a soccer star. People still knew and loved Sánchez for his great plays as a forward. He would always be listed among the soccer greats.

Fans still haven't forgotten the soccer superstar of the 1980s and '90s.

CHAPTER 5

In the News

Just about everybody in Mexico knows who Hugo Sánchez is. Through his careers on the field and in coaching, he's made big news. Sánchez has made some tough decisions and scored some amazing goals. Each one lands him in front of dozens of reporters and in newspapers and television news shows around the world. Through it all, though, fans know that he is one of the best Mexican soccer players ever.

WORLDWIDE FAME

Sánchez's career has stretched around the globe. He has fans in Mexico, South America, the United States, and Europe.

Many fans believe Sánchez is one of the best players ever to come out of Mexico. He is even listed on the International Federation of Association Football (FIFA) top 100 list. He's also listed as the twenty-sixth-best player in the twentieth century. That's quite an honor!

Recently, Hugo Sánchez was also named as the one player that shows the "Sports **HERITAGE** of Humanity." Hundreds of thousands of people from seventy-two countries voted. Out of a list of forty players, they picked Sánchez. Voters thought he was a great voice for world soccer and wanted to remember him for decades to come.

To top it all off, Sánchez has also won a Golden Foot. The award is given to players who are at least twenty-nine, and who have done big things in soccer. Players can only win it once in their lives. Sánchez won the award in 2010.

CONTROVERSIES

From time to time, Sánchez gets in the middle of a **CONTROVERSY.** He often says exactly what he thinks. Sometimes, that gets him in trouble.

Sometimes Sánchez even gets in trouble for things he never said! For example, some said Sánchez had been talking badly about Venezuelan soccer. People got upset and started attacking Sánchez.

Sánchez isn't going anywhere yet! Fans haven't seen the last of him.

Even though he was blamed for it, however, Sánchez never actually said anything bad about Venezuela. The damage had already been done, though. Many Venezuelan fans started to hate Sánchez.

Sánchez is also known for his famous fight with Ricardo La Volpe, another Mexican coach. Sánchez didn't agree with how La Volpe coached the Mexican national team. He didn't like anything else about La Volpe, either. Neither coach liked the other.

The fight with La Volpe started in 1979. Sánchez scored six goals in just

The Great Fox

Ricardo La Volpe is known as the Great Fox. He was born in Argentina, but has worked with soccer teams in many different countries. He first played on the Argentinian team that won the World Cup, and later went on to coach the Mexican national team. Later he worked in Costa Rica. La Volpe can sometimes have a short temper, but most people agree that he's a great coach!

Hugo Sánchez is a soccer icon to Mexican fans.

Though Sánchez can be a controversial figure from time to time, many people agree that he's the best Mexican soccer player ever to take the field.

two games. After the first three, La Volpe told the press that it was just luck. He didn't think Sánchez was actually a good player. La Volpe also claimed that it would never happen again. Of course, Sánchez did score three more goals, proving him wrong.

Twenty years later, Sánchez started playing for Club Atlante in Mexico. La Volpe was the coach. Something was bound to go wrong between the two soccer stars.

Player Felix Fernandez saw what happened next. He talked about how the two men got into an argument over something very little. But the argument got bigger and bigger. Fernandez said, "I saw La Volpe jumping onto Hugo, wrapping his hands around his neck. Hugo didn't resist at all...They argued violently for several minutes, an inch away one from the other. Then they split ways and everyone wondered what had happened. The only broke thing was Hugo's watch."

Fans are always excited to read the latest insults traded by the two star coaches.

Whether it's an amazing goal, a coaching win, or even a fight with another coach, people love to watch whatever Hugo Sánchez does next. He's a true soccer **ICON** and has proven again and again that he has earned the title of the best Mexican player in history.

Though he's had some ups and downs, Hugo Sánchez's career has been amazing to watch. The Pentapichichi earned a place in international soccer history.

FIND OUT MORE

On the Internet

123 FOOTBALL

www.123football.com/players/s/hugo-Sánchez

BIOGRAPHY BASE

www.biographybase.com/biography/Sánchez_hugo.html

ESPN.COM SOCCER NEWS

espn.go.com/sports/soccer

FIFA.COM MEXICO

www.fifa.com/associations/association=mex/index.html

GOAL.COM MEXICAN SOCCER NEWS

www.goal.com/en-us/news/114/mexico

SOCCERFANSINFO.COM

www.soccer-fans-info.com/hugo-Sánchez.html

GLOSSARY

CHAMPIONSHIPS: Competitions between two soccer teams to choose a winner of a league or division.

CONTROVERSY: An argument around something people have different opinions about.

FORWARDS: Soccer players who play closest to the other team's goal, trying to score goals.

HERITAGE: Tradition or history.

INJURIES: Pains or hurt body parts that force a player to take a break from the sport.

OFF-SEASON: The time between sports seasons.

PROFESSIONAL: Professionals are paid for their work.

QUALIFYING: Qualifying matches are games played to see which team can move on to play in a tournament or competition.

RETIRE: To end a career.

TOURNAMENT: A series of games played to choose a winner.

INDEX